THE UNITED STATES AND MEXICO

BY NEL YOMTOV

CHILDREN'S PRESS®
An Imprint of Scholastic Inc.
New York Toronto London Auckland Sydney
Mexico City New Delhi Hong Kong
Danbury, Connecticut

BRINGING HISTORY to LIFE

Content Consultant
James Marten, PhD
Professor and Chair, History Department
Marquette University
Milwaukee, Wisconsin

Library of Congress Cataloging-in-Publication Data
Yomtov, Nelson.
  The United States and Mexico / by Nel Yomtov.
    p. cm.—(Cornerstones of freedom)
  Includes bibliographical references and index.
  ISBN 978-0-531-23605-5 (library binding)—ISBN 978-0-531-21963-8 (pbk.)
1. United States—Foreign relations—Mexico—Juvenile literature. 2.
Mexico—Foreign relations—United States—Juvenile
literature. I. Title.
  E183.8.M6Y66 2013
  327.73072—dc23   2012034324

1 2 3 4 5 6 7 8 9 10 R 22 21 20 19 18 17 16 15 14 13

Photographs © 2013: Alamy Images/Frank Paul: 5 bottom, 35; AP Images:
7 (Denis Poroy), 42 (Doug Mills), 41 (Lennox McLendon), 55 (Wilfredo
Lee), 36, 38; Bridgeman Art Library/William Holl: 12, 56 top; Corbis Images/
Bettmann: 39, 40; Getty Images: 44 (Bertrand Langlois/AFP), 33 (Hulton
Archive), 46 (Joe Raedle), back cover (Marcos Ferro), 54 (Susana
Gonzalez/Bloomberg); Inland Valley Daily Bulletin/Will Lester: cover;
Library of Congress: 30, 31 (Bain News Service), 13 (C. Seiler), 4 bottom,
25 (John Chester Buttre); Newscom: 49 (Alejandro Zepeda/EPA), 43 (Les
Stone/ZUMA Press), 51 (ZUMA Press); Shutterstock, Inc./Olinchuk: 5 top,
6; Superstock, Inc./Frederick Catherwood/Newberry Library: 16; The Art
Archive/Picture Desk/Museo de America Madrid/Gianni Dagli Orti: 8; The
Granger Collection: 18, 56 bottom (Henry Arthur McArdle), 15 (Rembrandt
Peale), 2, 3, 23 (ullstein bild), 4 top, 10, 21, 26, 28.

Maps by XNR Productions, Inc.

Did you know that studying history can be fun?

BRING HISTORY TO LIFE by becoming a history investigator. Examine the evidence (primary and secondary source materials); cross-examine the people and witnesses. Take a look at what was happening at the time—but be careful! What happened years ago might suddenly become incredibly interesting and change the way you think!

Contents

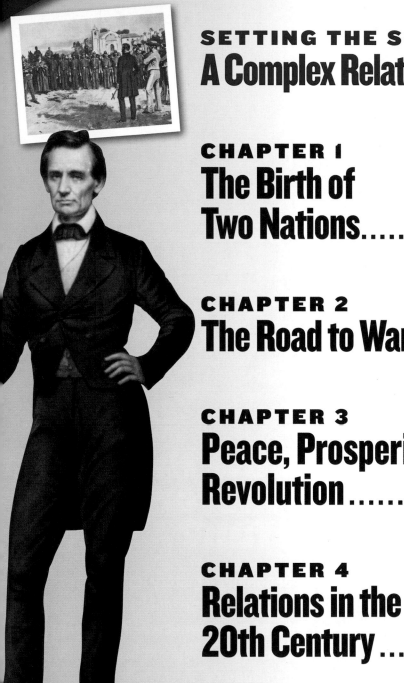

4

A Complex Relationship

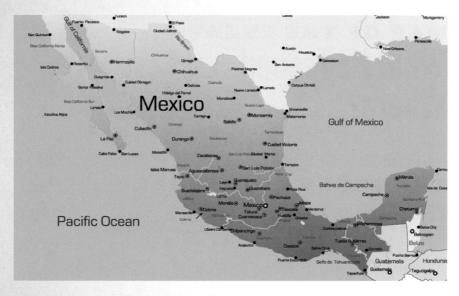

Mexico lies directly south of the United States along the western half of the country.

The 1,950-mile-long (3,138-kilometer) border that separates the United States from Mexico is not just a political boundary. It also divides two vastly different cultures. To the north, the United States is known for its wealth and political stability. To the south, Mexico

MEXICO HAS A POPULATION

remains largely underdeveloped and comparatively poor. Mexico also has a long history of political chaos.

Despite their differences, these two neighbors share strong **economic**, cultural, and historic ties. But the imbalance in wealth and political power has created a complicated relationship between the two nations. Many Americans believe that Mexico is an inferior nation because of its longtime economic and political dependence on the United States. In Mexico, many people believe that the United States has unfairly dominated its southern neighbor.

Since the mid-19th century, the United States has often interfered in Mexican affairs. For instance, one of the most devastating events in Mexican history was the loss of almost half the nation's territory following the U.S. victory in the Mexican-American War (1846–1848). Such occurrences have fueled feelings of mistrust and suspicion of America among the people of Mexico.

U.S. and Mexican security forces ensure that people do not pass freely between the two countries without proper authorization.

OF ALMOST 115 MILLION PEOPLE.

CHAPTER 1

THE BIRTH OF TWO NATIONS

Spanish colonists found great economic success in North America.

FROM THE EARLY 16TH CENTURY to the early 19th century, the area that would become Mexico was a Spanish colony. This territory, called New Spain, enriched its mother country with valuable minerals and other raw materials.

In the early 17th century, England established its own colonies along the east coast of North America. These settlements quickly developed thriving **agricultural** and trade-based economies. For many years, there was little contact between the colonies of Spain and England. By the 19th century, however, the colonists' descendants in Mexico and the United States were on a rocky path toward war.

Spanish explorer Hernán Cortés and his men used their powerful weapons to defeat the Aztec and take over Tenochtitlán.

Ancient Mexico

Before the Spaniards arrived, the lands of ancient Mexico were home to many native civilizations. Among these cultures were the Maya, the Toltec, and the Zapotec. The Aztec were the final native people to arrive in the region. Their legends claim that they came from a mythical place north of Mexico in about 1000 CE.

In the early 1300s, the Aztec settled in the swampy islands around present-day Mexico City. There they built the magnificent capital city of Tenochtitlán. By the early 16th century, the powerful Aztec Empire dominated most of central and southern Mexico.

The Spanish Conquest

At that time, Spain had established colonies on islands in the Caribbean Sea. Motivated by tales of Aztec wealth, Spanish adventurer Hernán Cortés organized a fleet of ships and stocked them with more than 600 men and plenty of guns and ammunition. In 1519, he sailed from Cuba to Mexico. Cortés and his men arrested the Aztec emperor Montezuma II and took control of Tenochtitlán.

A revolt led by Aztec chieftains forced the Spaniards to retreat eastward from the city. However, the Spaniards had inadvertently carried the deadly disease smallpox with them to Mexico. An outbreak of this illness killed off much of the Aztec population in Tenochtitlán. With his enemy weakened, Cortés returned to conquer the city in the summer of 1521. After three weeks of bloody combat, the Spaniards used their superior firepower to take control of Tenochtitlán.

One by one, local towns surrendered to the Spaniards. The capital of New Spain was built on top of the ruins of Tenochtitlán and renamed Mexico City.

Cortés gave his men land and forced native people to serve as unpaid labor. The promises of riches to be found in New Spain attracted large numbers of Spaniards and other Europeans to the new colony. African slaves were soon sent to work the land alongside the native people.

The English Colonies

In 1607, English colonists established Jamestown, the first permanent English settlement in North America.

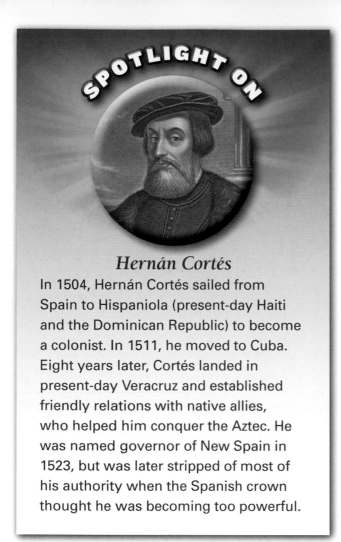

Hernán Cortés

In 1504, Hernán Cortés sailed from Spain to Hispaniola (present-day Haiti and the Dominican Republic) to become a colonist. In 1511, he moved to Cuba. Eight years later, Cortés landed in present-day Veracruz and established friendly relations with native allies, who helped him conquer the Aztec. He was named governor of New Spain in 1523, but was later stripped of most of his authority when the Spanish crown thought he was becoming too powerful.

Over the next several decades, its success led to the formation and growth of many more English colonies along the East Coast.

Between 1754 and 1763, British forces battled France and its Native American allies for control of a large portion of North America. The conflict, called the French and Indian War, resulted in victory for the British. Soon afterward, the British government forced new taxes on its colonists to help pay for the war. The colonists objected on the grounds that they had no representation in Parliament, England's body of lawmakers. In 1775, hostilities erupted between colonists and British soldiers stationed in the colonies. On July 4, 1776, the 13 colonies declared their independence from England.

With help from France and, to a lesser degree, Spain, the colonists won their independence from England in the Revolutionary War (1775–1783). The Treaty of Paris officially ended the war. It set the boundaries of the

In 1807, American explorer Zebulon Pike published a map titled "A Map of the Internal Provinces of New Spain." The map shows many Spanish-controlled territories, from the Gulf of Mexico in the east to the Colorado River in the west. See page 60 for a link to view a copy of Pike's original map online.

newly formed United States as Canada to the north and northwest and New Spain to the south and west. England also gave Spain its territories in Florida, though no definite boundaries were established there.

Spain's Reaction to American Independence

The birth of the new nation brought it into immediate contact with its southern neighbor. In 1795, Spain signed the

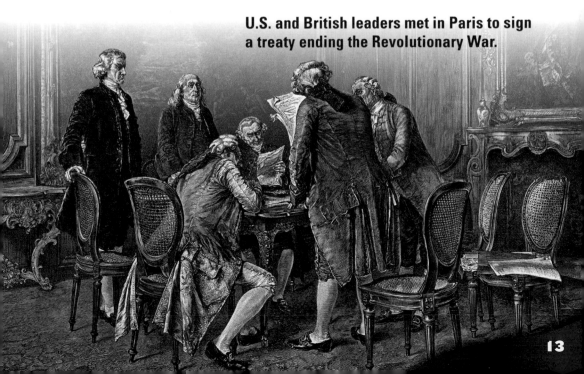

U.S. and British leaders met in Paris to sign a treaty ending the Revolutionary War.

Treaty of San Lorenzo with the United States. It recognized the U.S. borders at the Mississippi River and along the northern edge of Florida. The treaty also allowed American goods to be transported free of charge through the Spanish-held port of New Orleans. This gave American farmers in western states such as Mississippi, Ohio, and Kentucky access to waterways that led to markets in the East.

When French emperor Napoleon Bonaparte invaded Spain in 1808, several Spanish colonies in America declared themselves independent. The United States took further advantage of Spain's troubles with France and **annexed** part of Florida in 1810.

In 1818, a disagreement over the border separating the United States and New Spain erupted. The United States insisted that the border be farther south into Spanish territory, but Spain wanted it established farther north. The matter was somewhat settled when the U.S. Army invaded eastern Florida and convinced Spain to sell that territory to the United States. In exchange, the United States agreed to compromise on the border. The price for eastern Florida was set at $5 million, but the United States never paid.

Independence for New Spain

In the early 1800s, anger toward Spanish control in New Spain swelled into a revolutionary movement. The goal of the movement was to establish a more balanced social structure, eliminate slavery, and distribute land to the common people. Revolutionary forces battled Spanish armies throughout New Spain.

Success seemed to come in 1812 when the Spanish government agreed to a new constitution guaranteeing certain freedoms to all of its subjects. Two years later, however, the king of Spain rejected the new constitution and assumed complete control of New Spain.

Civil war broke out and raged for almost 10 years as revolutionaries in New Spain fought for control of the colony's government. As the revolution gained strength, rebel forces banded together throughout Mexico. In September 1821, the Spanish crown recognized Mexican independence. New Spain became the Mexican Empire.

YESTERDAY'S HEADLINES

After Mexico achieved independence, nations around the world feared that Spain would try to reestablish its authority in Mexico. The United States grew concerned that a war in the region would threaten its own safety. In December 1823, President James Monroe (above) warned European nations not to interfere in the Western Hemisphere. "The American continents . . . are henceforth not to be considered as subjects for future colonization by any European powers," he said. His statement became known as the Monroe Doctrine, and it became the foundation of future U.S. foreign policy.

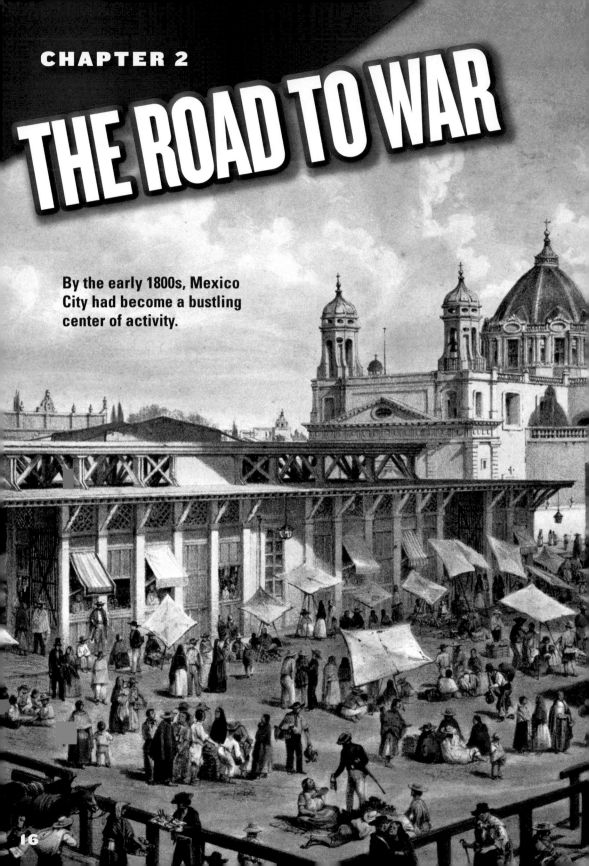

CHAPTER 2
THE ROAD TO WAR

By the early 1800s, Mexico City had become a bustling center of activity.

MEXICO WAS NOW THE LARGEST nation in the Western Hemisphere. But the country was in **debt** to Spain, and its mining, trade, and agricultural activities had been devastated by years of civil war. Mexico was still politically unsettled and had to rely on foreign nations for goods and loans. The United States eyed its southern neighbor's weakened condition as an opportunity to expand its own borders.

Stephen F. Austin (center) led one of the first groups of Americans to settle in Texas.

The Question of Texas

Until the 19th century, the northern territory of Mexico (including present-day Texas) was sparsely settled. After the Louisiana Purchase in 1803, however, Americans began flocking to Texas. Many brought their slaves with them. By 1835, the **immigrant** and slave population in Texas would be about twice as large as the Mexican population.

Hoping to attract settlers to Texas, the Mexican government granted colonies to settlers from such nations as the United States, Germany, and Switzerland.

One of the most famous colonies was founded by Moses Austin of Missouri. Austin was given permission to settle a colony of 300 families. He died before he could establish the colony, but his son Stephen went to Texas in his place in 1821. Stephen F. Austin was given broad powers to govern the new colony.

The Spanish Colonization Act had granted Austin lands. It also placed certain restrictions on the new colonists. Colonizers had to be Catholic, and they were not allowed to settle on the coast or near the border. The Imperial Colonization Law, another law aimed at new settlers, allowed slaves to be brought into Texas but banned their sale.

The settlers ignored all these restrictions. They were far from the reaches of the government in Mexico City and preferred to keep close ties to the United States. So when Mexico outlawed slavery in 1829, the Texans simply paid no attention to the new law. They also demanded the removal of certain taxes placed on them by the Mexican government.

Mexico Takes a Stand

In 1830, the Mexican government passed a law that banned additional Americans from settling in Texas. The Mexican leader, General Antonio López de Santa Anna, took a hard stand against the Texans. He also refused to give in to any of the Texans' demands. In 1835, he took away the right to self-government that had been granted to Stephen F. Austin.

In February 1836, Santa Anna and his troops made their way north into the heart of Texas, arriving in San Antonio. There they began the **siege** of the Alamo, a former church where about 180 rebels had sought safety to make a final stand. By the time the fighting was over, everyone in the Alamo had been killed.

A few weeks later, on March 2, Texas declared independence from Mexico and formed a **republic**, naming Sam Houston head of the military. Bands of Texans seized control of several Mexican towns, including the city of San Antonio. The Texas Revolution had begun.

In late March, another violent massacre occurred. Mexican troops forced a Texan army of about 330 men to surrender in the city of Goliad. On direct orders from Santa Anna, the entire force was executed.

The Texans' Victory

Sam Houston retreated east, with Santa Anna's army in close pursuit. The events at the Alamo and Goliad had whipped up strong anti-Mexican feelings in the United States. Volunteer fighters stormed into Texas eager to crush Santa Anna's forces. The U.S. government supported their cause with guns, ammunition, and money.

On April 21, 1836, a force led by Houston ambushed and defeated Santa Anna and his army at the San Jacinto River. Two days later, Santa Anna was captured. While imprisoned, he agreed to end the hostilities and recognize Texan independence from Mexico. The Lone Star Republic of Texas was born.

Prelude to War

The United States recognized Texas's independence in March 1837. Soon afterward, many Americans began calling for the U.S. government to annex Texas. They believed that it was the fate of the United States to control North America, a concept that became known as Manifest Destiny. However, Mexico warned that if the United States annexed Texas, it would declare war.

In 1844, James K. Polk was elected president. Polk was a strong supporter of Manifest Destiny. He openly desired to annex Texas, even if it meant going to war with Mexico. In February 1845, Congress agreed to offer the new republic statehood. The Texans accepted the offer on July 4, and Texas was annexed into the Union on December 29.

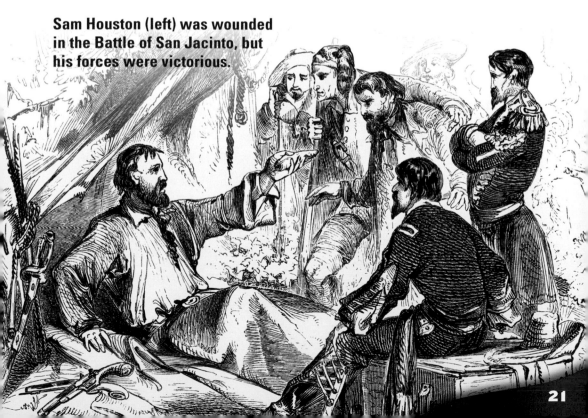

Sam Houston (left) was wounded in the Battle of San Jacinto, but his forces were victorious.

Polk then made plans to protect the Texas frontier. Before being annexed, the Texans had claimed their southern border with Mexico to be the Rio Grande. However, Mexico firmly declared that the border stood at the Nueces River, about 150 miles (241 km) north of the Rio Grande. Polk gave orders to diplomat John Slidell to negotiate with Mexico to set the boundary at the Rio Grande.

In January 1846, Polk sent General Zachary Taylor and his army to Texas in case Mexico refused to cooperate with Slidell. Taylor positioned his men north of the Rio Grande. The Mexican army observed the activities of the U.S. forces from the south bank of the river. On April 25, fighting broke out between the two sides. Several U.S.

A VIEW FROM ABROAD

Great Britain was opposed to the U.S. annexation of the Republic of Texas. Its leaders wanted to halt the westward expansion of the United States and continue benefiting from the trade relationships they had already established with Texas. The British advised the Mexican government to recognize the independence of Texas on the condition that Texas refuse any offer of annexation made by the United States. Given the choice between annexation and recognition of independence by Mexico, the Texans chose annexation.

The United States was victorious in the Battle of Cerro Gordo.

soldiers were killed. Polk reported the news to Congress, and a declaration of war on Mexico was quickly approved.

The Mexican-American War

The United States attacked Mexico in three areas: California and New Mexico; northern Mexico; and Veracruz, in southern Mexico on the Gulf Coast. In August 1846, U.S. forces took Santa Fe, New Mexico, without a fight. By early 1847, California had also fallen to American control. In February 1847, General Zachary Taylor defeated Santa Anna in a fierce fight at Buena Vista, in northern Mexico.

In March 1847, General Winfield Scott's forces landed at Veracruz. A heavy bombardment from U.S.

ships stationed off the coast forced the city to surrender. After fighting past Cerro Gordo, Scott's forces marched toward Mexico City, where combat lasted from August to September. On September 13, the last gasp of Mexican resistance was crushed at the Battle of Chapultepec. The war was over, and negotiations for peace began.

The Treaty of Guadalupe Hidalgo

The Treaty of Guadalupe Hidalgo was signed on February 2, 1848. It was another humiliation suffered by Mexico at the hands of the United States. The treaty called for the border between the two nations to be set at the Rio Grande. Mexico also turned over to the United States the lands of New Mexico and northern California (present-day California, Utah, Nevada, Colorado, Wyoming, New Mexico, and parts of Oklahoma and Arizona). In return, the United States agreed to pay $15 million.

This loss of land was a devastating blow to Mexico. In 1849, just one year after the treaty was signed, gold

A FIRSTHAND LOOK AT
THE TREATY OF GUADALUPE HIDALGO

The Treaty of Guadalupe Hidalgo, which ended the Mexican-American War, awarded the United States more than 500,000 square miles (1.3 million square kilometers) of land, about one-sixth of the present-day continental United States. See page 60 for a link to view the original treaty, written in English and Spanish.

was discovered in California. By 1870, the lost territories were producing vast amounts of valuable minerals. U.S. success in these new territories quickly widened the economic gap between the United States and Mexico. Mexico's losses fueled a mistrust of the United States and set the pattern for the complicated relationship that exists to this day.

In 1854, Santa Anna sold land in southern New Mexico and Arizona to the United States for $10 million in a deal known as the Gadsden Purchase. Many Mexicans were outraged over another sale of land to the Americans. They rebelled against Santa Anna and drove him from power in 1855.

YESTERDAY'S HEADLINES

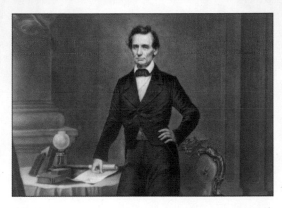

Abraham Lincoln (above) was one of the most outspoken critics of the Mexican-American War. He believed the war was unconstitutional and unnecessary. After President Polk sent U.S. troops to the Rio Grande, Lincoln, then serving in the House of Representatives, wrote a letter to a friend in February 1848. "Allow the President to invade a neighboring nation, whenever he shall deem it necessary to repel an invasion, and you allow him to do so, whenever he may choose to say he deems it necessary for such purpose and you allow him to make war at pleasure," he wrote.

CHAPTER 3

PEACE, PROSPERITY ...AND REVOLUTION

Benito Juárez was elected the president of Mexico in 1861.

BENITO JUÁREZ REPLACED

Santa Anna as Mexico's leader. Juárez aimed to revive Mexico's ruined economy and bring liberty to Mexicans of all classes. Under his directions, the government took control of lands owned by the Catholic Church. Special rights for priests and members of the army were eliminated. The nation, however, was nearly out of money. Mexico was unable to pay back the money it had borrowed from foreign countries in previous decades. In 1862, England, France, and Spain invaded Mexico to take control of its ports and get their money back. England and France eventually withdrew, but France had larger goals in mind.

Archduke Maximilian of Austria was executed by a firing squad.

Mexico Gets U.S. Support

Hoping to reestablish France's presence in America, Emperor Napoleon III of France installed Archduke Maximilian of Austria as emperor of Mexico. With the United States engaged in the Civil War (1861–1865), France ignored the Monroe Doctrine, which warned foreign nations to stay out of the Western Hemisphere. The United States was unable to give Juárez financial or military support because its resources were being used to fight the war at home.

When the Civil War ended, the United States turned its attention to France and Mexico. The U.S. government demanded that France give up its plans of building an empire in America. To back up these demands, the United States sent troops to the Mexican border. It also provided

Juárez with the modern weapons it had used in the Civil War. In May 1867, Mexican rebels defeated Maximilian's troops in the city of Querétaro. The emperor was tried by a court and executed. Juárez was restored to power.

Porfirio Díaz Seizes Power

Juárez died in office in 1872. Four years later, Porfirio Díaz took power. Díaz had fought against the French. He would hold power for 35 years. During that time, he reshaped Mexico's economy, politics, and military.

Díaz healed the Mexican government's relations with the Catholic Church and returned the property that had been taken during the Juárez era. He also built a powerful military force and took firm control of the government and the economy. Mexico was slowly turning from a republic into a **dictatorship**.

Díaz brought stability to Mexico, which made it desirable to foreign investors. He allowed these investors to develop millions of acres of land that had been taken from native Indians. This created a surge in Mexico's mining industry. As the country became **industrialized**, trade between Mexico and the United States boomed. Mexico **exported** products from its mines, farms, and forests. U.S. companies sent Mexico machinery and tools.

American Investment in the Díaz Regime

Díaz also changed Mexico's land ownership policy. Under Spanish control, the government had owned

Porfirio Díaz's efforts to transform Mexico into a modern nation came at the expense of eliminating the influence of its traditional culture. Díaz is said to have painted his face to make it look whiter than it actually was. He did this to make himself look more European. Díaz and the wealthy upper class of Mexico prospered as he sold off the rights to Mexico's natural resources and industries to foreign investors. By the time he was forced from power, foreign business interests owned most of Mexico's oil fields, railways, and mills.

all mineral wealth that lay beneath the surface of the ground. The owner of the land had rights only to its surface. Díaz gave U.S. oil companies subsoil ownership. This meant that whatever was pumped out of the ground belonged to the company.

By 1911, Mexico had become the world's third-largest producer of oil. But U.S. companies, such as the Standard Oil Company and Texaco, controlled nearly 50 percent of Mexico's oil. U.S. interests also controlled about 75 percent of Mexico's other mineral resources and a large portion of its agricultural production.

Mexican workers suffered under Díaz and foreign control. The billions of dollars of foreign investment went to the government and the upper class. Miners and factory workers had no political rights. They worked long hours for low pay. Education and public health services were nearly nonexistent. Once again, Mexico was ripe for revolution.

The Revolution Begins

In Mexico's 1910 presidential election, Francisco Madero, the son of a wealthy industrialist, announced that he would run against Díaz. Madero claimed that he would eliminate corruption and inequality in the government. Díaz had Madero arrested

Francisco Madero was president of Mexico from 1911 until his assassination in 1913.

and then jailed him until the election. Madero escaped and fled to San Antonio, Texas, where he plotted to overthrow Díaz.

On November 20, 1910, Madero and armed groups of supporters fought several small battles with Díaz's army in Mexico. Although they were beaten back, and Madero was forced to return to the United States, many new followers joined the cause.

Leaders of other anti-Díaz rebel groups included Francisco "Pancho" Villa and Emiliano Zapata. By May 1911, the combined forces of Madero, Villa, and Zapata defeated Díaz's troops. The dictator was forced to resign and flee to Europe. Madero was elected president in October. He appointed Victoriano Huerta, a Díaz general, to lead the defense of his new government.

The United States Intervenes

Meanwhile, the U.S. government grew concerned about the safety of American investments in Mexico. American investors feared that the changes in the Mexican government would topple the financial empires they had built.

In 1913, supporters of Victoriano Huerta murdered Madero and the vice president. Huerta's violent takeover threw Mexico into civil war. The United States opposed his military dictatorship. So did revolutionaries Zapata and Villa. South of Mexico City, Zapata's peasant army destroyed the large farms of wealthy Huerta supporters. In the north, Villa and his bands of rebels attacked wealthy landowners and government military outposts.

Pancho Villa and Emiliano Zapata rallied Mexican farmers and peasants to form large armies.

New groups of rebels soon formed throughout Mexico, including an 8,000-man army under Álvaro Obregón, a farmer and politician. Venustiano Carranza, the governor of a Mexican province, and his Constitutionalist Army also rallied against Huerta. Though they had once supported Huerta, U.S. oil interests gave financial backing to the rebels.

After learning that a German ship was heading toward the port of Veracruz with weapons for Huerta, President Woodrow Wilson ordered 800 troops to occupy the city and ready themselves for a march into Mexico City if Huerta refused to resign. The U.S. Navy captured Veracruz, killing more than 200 Mexicans.

With pressure from internal rebel groups and the U.S. military preparing to invade his capital city, Huerta resigned in July 1914.

Border Wars

Rebel forces immediately split into warring factions after Huerta's departure. Obregón and Carranza teamed up. They were opposed by Villa, Zapata, and other revolutionary leaders who operated in different parts of Mexico.

World War I (1914–1918) had begun in Europe. The United States needed an ally in Mexico who could stabilize the country's economy and restore order to the government. President Wilson believed that Villa was the right person for the job. Villa had financed his revolutionary activities by seizing only lands owned by Mexicans. He had left American-owned property alone.

At the end of 1914, however, Villa suffered a series of heavy losses against Carranza's forces. When the United States turned over Veracruz to Carranza, who had become head of the Mexican government, Villa took action against the Americans.

In March 1916, Villa and his army crossed the border and attacked the village of Columbus, New Mexico. Several Americans were killed in the attack. President

Wilson sent an army of 6,000 troops into Mexico to capture Villa, but they were unsuccessful.

The Constitution of 1917

Carranza's most lasting legacy was the Mexican constitution of 1917. It guaranteed rights for workers, established a system of public education, and limited the nonreligious powers of the Catholic Church.

The constitution reestablished the principle that subsoil rights belonged to Mexico. Resources that lay beneath the land's surface could be tapped only under strict terms set by the Mexican government. The constitution also gave the government the power to seize and redistribute land at will.

SPOTLIGHT ON

The Mexican Civil War and U.S. Military Development

The use of U.S. troops during the Mexican Revolution helped the United States develop its own military readiness. The navy and marine operations at Veracruz and the mission to hunt Villa laid the groundwork for resources that the United States used in World War I. U.S. activities in Mexico allowed the military to conduct training exercises, improve its weaponry, and develop spy networks. The mission to find Villa even featured one of the first wartime uses of airplanes. By 1918, improved models of those planes were being used in combat in France.

CHAPTER 4

RELATIONS IN THE 20TH CENTURY

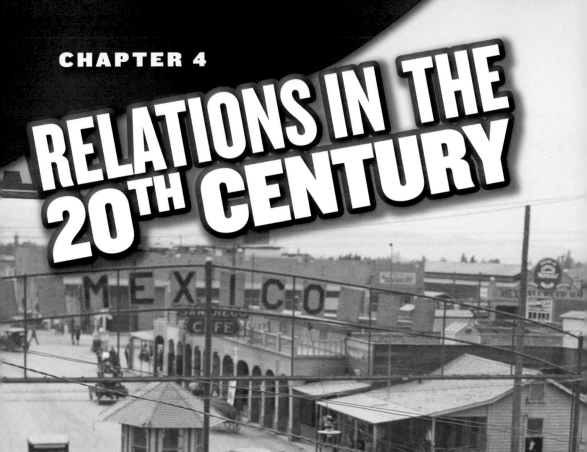

During the 1920s, the U.S. government set up border checkpoints to prevent Mexicans from entering the United States.

IN THE LATE 19TH CENTURY, large numbers of Mexicans began migrating to the United States. They came in search of employment opportunities on farms, ranches, and railroads in the West and along the border. Later, they came to work in factories and on farms to meet America's labor needs during World War I. In the 1920s, many Americans began objecting to the large influx of immigrants. The U.S. Border Patrol was established to end the easy crossing between Mexico and the United States. This action deepened anti-American feelings in Mexico.

Hundreds of thousands of Mexicans gathered to celebrate Mexico's regaining ownership of its oil.

Mexico Takes Control

In May 1937, Mexican oil workers went on strike to demand higher wages. The oil companies did not want to bargain with the workers. Mexican president Lázaro Cárdenas stepped in to settle the dispute.

In 1938, Cárdenas proclaimed that he would seize all foreign oil holdings, as allowed by the constitution of 1917. The American oil companies urged the U.S. government to take swift action. But President Franklin D. Roosevelt recognized Mexico's rights. The two nations negotiated a settlement in which the oil companies were paid millions of dollars by the Mexican government. Mexico's oil, however, now belonged to Mexico.

The Second World War

With the outbreak of hostilities in Europe and the Pacific in the late 1930s, relations between the United States and Mexico warmed. From 1942 to 1945, the two nations were formal allies. They developed close military, political, and economic ties to fight the Axis powers of Germany, Italy, and Japan.

More than 16 million U.S. troops served in World War II.

Mexico's largest contribution to the war effort was its supply of raw materials and agricultural products. It also contributed labor to meet wartime needs in the United States. In 1942, the U.S. government established the Bracero Program. This program allowed contract workers, or braceros, into the United States to work for limited amounts of time. Roughly 300,000 Mexican workers were hired under the program during the war. At the same time, hundreds of thousands of immigrants were entering the United States illegally.

After the war, the U.S. government decided that the country did not need so many braceros and began sending them back to Mexico. Many Mexicans were angered that the United States had welcomed Mexicans when their labor was needed, but sent them away when their services were no longer necessary.

Braceros provided a valuable source of farm labor in the United States during World War II.

Immigration Concerns

In early 1981, Congress reported on the issue of illegal immigration into the United States. By that time, roughly 800,000 illegal Mexican immigrants were being held and returned by the Border Patrol each year. Ten years earlier, the number had been around 300,000.

The report claimed that the illegal immigrants were often treated poorly by American employers. These findings resulted in the 1986 Immigration Reform and Control Act. Legal citizenship was given to illegal immigrants who had entered the United States before January 1, 1982, and lived there continuously. American

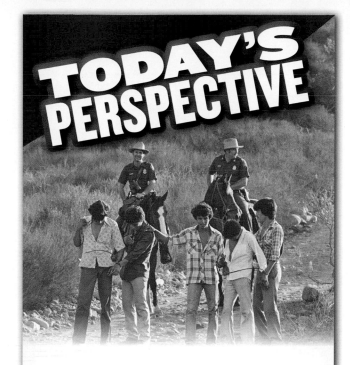

TODAY'S PERSPECTIVE

Did the Immigration Reform and Control Act of 1986 ease the flow of illegal immigrants into the United States? For six months after the law went into effect, there was a slowdown of illegal immigration. However, it shortly returned to normal levels and then increased. One problem with the act was that once illegal immigrants were in the United States and meeting certain requirements, they were put on a path to U.S. citizenship immediately. Law-abiding applicants had to wait in Mexico for years just to get the **visas** required to enter the United States. This encouraged Mexicans hoping to immigrate to choose the illegal path instead of the legal one.

President Bill Clinton signed NAFTA into law on December 8, 1993.

employers were banned from knowingly hiring illegal immigrants and could be fined for doing so. However, tracking down illegal Mexican immigrants was a difficult task. Their numbers continued to swell.

Opening the Door to Free Trade

Mexico experienced economic hardships in the 1980s. Oil prices dropped rapidly. **Inflation** and unemployment rose to frightening levels. The United States believed that a trade agreement between the two nations would help open and stabilize Mexico's economy. After much debate, the North American Free Trade Agreement (NAFTA) went into effect on January 1, 1994. The agreement was designed to eliminate **tariffs** and thereby encourage trade among Canada, Mexico, and the United

States. Tariffs on more than one-half of Mexico's exports to the United States and more than one-third of U.S. exports to Mexico were immediately lifted.

The early effects of the agreement were encouraging. Investors spent billions of dollars developing manufacturing facilities and modernizing farming operations in Mexico. But not all of the results were positive. Some Mexican industries collapsed, because many of the huge companies that came to Mexico used parts from their own suppliers rather than from Mexican companies. Local farmers were often unable to compete with food that was **imported** tariff-free. Unemployed Mexicans crossed into the United States seeking work.

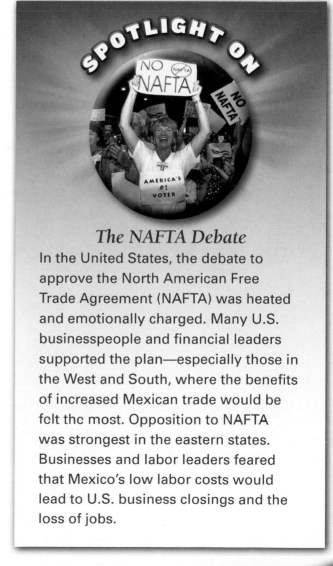

The NAFTA Debate

In the United States, the debate to approve the North American Free Trade Agreement (NAFTA) was heated and emotionally charged. Many U.S. businesspeople and financial leaders supported the plan—especially those in the West and South, where the benefits of increased Mexican trade would be felt the most. Opposition to NAFTA was strongest in the eastern states. Businesses and labor leaders feared that Mexico's low labor costs would lead to U.S. business closings and the loss of jobs.

CHAPTER 5

THE UNITED STATES AND MEXICO TODAY

U.S. president Barack Obama (left) and Mexican president Felipe Calderón (right) met with other world leaders to discuss economic issues at the 2012 G20 summit in Mexico.

DESPITE THE MANY

disagreements between Mexico and the United States, both nations have maintained similar goals in their relationship. Mexican leaders desire political stability and economic growth. They seek the cooperation of the United States to achieve these objectives. The United States hopes for Mexico's political and social stability and its economic development. The 21st century will test each nation's cooperative spirit as they address several important issues that affect the future of their relationship: trade, immigration, and drug trafficking.

The U.S. Border Patrol stops Mexicans from entering the United States illegally.

The Future of Mexican-American Trade

Many observers agree that NAFTA has had a positive effect in increasing trade among its member countries. Mexican exports to the United States jumped from $40 billion in 1993 to $211 billion in 2007. Mexican imports from the United States soared from $41 billion to $136 billion during the same time period.

Mexican and U.S. leaders claimed another positive outcome would be that NAFTA would reduce illegal immigration to the United States because Mexicans would find plenty of work manufacturing goods in their home country. However, U.S. fears that jobs would be lost at home have been supported by a study conducted by the Economic Policy Institute. It claims that as of 2010, NAFTA has cost the United States roughly 680,000 jobs.

By 2012, the trade benefits of NAFTA had dwindled. But the positive changes in the relationship between Mexico and the United States continue to be felt. Mexico has more direct communication with U.S. politicians. Businesspeople from both countries now deal with each other more directly without the intervention of Mexican and U.S. lawmakers.

NAFTA faces an uncertain future. Many people on both sides of the border believe the agreement needs to be improved. Many others think that it should be canceled altogether.

Immigration

Mexican immigration to the United States began to drop in mid-2006, and this decline continued for several years. By March 2009, roughly 175,000 immigrants came from Mexico annually. That was about half the number of immigrants from the previous two years. By 2011, illegal immigration from Mexico was at its lowest level in 60 years.

One reason for the reversal has been the United States' sluggish economy. For the first time in years, many Mexicans believe they have a better chance of finding employment at home. Stronger U.S. law enforcement along the border is another reason for the dwindling numbers of illegal immigrants.

A VIEW FROM ABROAD

Mexican officials were outraged by SB 1070, Arizona's illegal immigration law. President Felipe Calderón condemned it as a "violation of human rights." The governor of Baja California, José Osuna Millán, claimed the law "could disrupt the indispensable economic, political, and cultural exchanges of the entire border region." The Mexican Foreign Ministry issued an advisory to Mexicans who traveled, lived, or studied in Arizona that they "may be harassed and questioned without further cause at any time."

Tough new laws against illegal immigration might also have played a role in slowing down movement across the border. In 2010, Arizona enacted SB 1070. This law requires **aliens** age 14 or older who are in the United States for more than 30 days to register with the U.S. government. They are then given registration documents to carry at all times. This law made it illegal for them to be out in public without these documents.

In June 2012, the U.S. Supreme Court struck down the part of the law that required all immigrants to carry registration documents. However, the court upheld the part of the law that requires police to check the immigration status of any individual they stop for another reason and suspect is in the country illegally.

In June 2012, President Obama announced that illegal immigrants who came to the United States before age 16 would be allowed to remain in the country without fear of being **deported**. The policy will allow these individuals to work legally and obtain government-issued documents such as driver's licenses. It does not grant citizenship, however.

Mexican soldiers guard more than nine tons of illegal drugs taken from a drug cartel.

A FIRSTHAND LOOK AT
OPERATION INTERCEPT

In 1969, the launching of Operation Intercept at the Mexico-U.S. border made headlines across the United States and Mexico. See page 60 to view an October 3, 1969, *Wall Street Journal* article on the program.

The Drug Connection

The border between Mexico and the United States is home to a bustling northbound trade of illegal drugs. Government officials on both sides of the border believe drug trafficking is the most serious source of tension between the countries. The United States accuses Mexico of failing to stop the flow of illegal drugs. Mexico argues that the United States has not done enough to limit its own use of narcotics.

Both nations have tried over the years to halt the trafficking of drugs with a series of aggressive programs. In September 1969, the United States launched Operation Intercept, a program of vehicle inspections at the border. Mexico's Operation Condor, launched in the 1970s, doubled the size of Mexico's police force. To kill the crops, airplanes sprayed deadly herbicides on fields where drugs were grown.

One of the problems Mexico faces is the violence that accompanies its attempts to stop the drug industry. Well-organized groups of drug producers and shippers, called cartels, control the flow of drugs into the United States.

Armed with powerful weapons, the cartels compete to control the U.S. market. Thousands of police, military personnel, and civilians are killed each year by drug-related violence.

Many experts believe Mexico and the United States need to look beyond law enforcement as a solution to the problem. They claim the United States must examine the social causes that result in its high demand for drugs. Likewise, Mexico must solve its social problems, such as widespread poverty, that push many people into the drug trade.

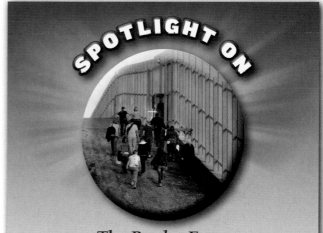

SPOTLIGHT ON

The Border Fence

In 2006, Congress passed the Secure Fence Act, a multibillion-dollar plan to build fence barriers across sections of the Mexico-U.S. border. The goal of the act is to slow the flow of drugs and illegal immigrants into the United States. It's difficult to determine how effective the barriers have been since they have been put up. In 2005, the U.S. Border Patrol caught roughly 1.2 million people trying to enter the United States illegally at the southwest border. By 2008, the number dwindled to around 705,000, and by 2010, it was around 448,000. The decrease in numbers may be a result of the slow U.S. economy or stronger border enforcements other than the fence.

What Happened Where?

Mexican land awarded to the U.S. under the Treaty of Guadalupe Hidalgo, 1848

Gadsden Purchase, 1853–1854

UNITED STATES

Annexed by U.S., 1845

Battle of
San Jacinto

Battle of the
Alamo

Battle of
Goliad

Battle of
Monterrey

N
W E
S

0   150   300 mi
0   150   300 km

MEXICO

Battle for Mexico City
Battle of Chapultepec

Battle of
Cerro Gordo
Siege of Veracruz

Many Mexicans work in large factories that produce goods for export to the United States and other countries.

The relationship between the United States and Mexico has often been a difficult one. Many Mexicans view their neighbor as a wealthy and powerful bully. Americans often think that Mexico depends too much on the United States and that illegal Mexican immigrants unfairly take advantage of America's wealth.

This relationship may be changing slowly toward one of greater equality between the two nations. In recent years, Mexico has reacted strongly when U.S. policies

AS OF 2012, MEXICAN BUSINESSMAN CARLOS

negatively affected its interests. In 2003, for example, Mexico took a bold step by resisting pressure to support the U.S. invasion of Iraq. And in 2007, it successfully influenced the United States to provide funds to fight the drug-related violence in Mexico.

Spurred by the trading partnership of NAFTA, Mexican and U.S. manufacturers and industrialists are building mutually beneficial trading relationships that will have a positive impact on both countries. These relationships may ultimately break down the walls of mistrust and suspicion that have existed between the two nations. History and geography make Mexico and the United States inseparable. Events that occur in the United States affect Mexico, and events in Mexico affect the United States. This mutual dependence binds the two nations together and will determine the nature of their relationship in the years ahead.

American and Mexican business leaders, such as Bill Gates (left) and Carlos Slim (right), work together to create new opportunities in both nations.

SLIM WAS THE RICHEST MAN IN THE WORLD.

INFLUENTIAL INDIVIDUALS

Hernán Cortés

Stephen F. Austin

Montezuma II (ca. 1466–1520) was the ruler of the Aztecs at the time of the Spanish conquest of Mexico.

Hernán Cortés (1485–1547) was a Spanish explorer who commanded the expedition that led to the fall of the Aztec Empire in 1521.

Zachary Taylor (1784–1850) was a major general in the U.S. Army during the Mexican-American War, where he led American forces to victory at the Battles of Palo Alto and Monterrey. In 1848, he was elected the 12th president of the United States.

Winfield Scott (1786–1866) was a U.S. military leader in the Mexican-American War. He captured Veracruz and marched on to Mexico City, where he helped defeat Santa Anna's forces.

Stephen F. Austin (1793–1836) established the first colony of Americans in the Texas province of Mexico.

Sam Houston (1793–1863) was the commander in chief of the Texas armies and the first president of the Texas Republic. His victory over Santa Anna at the Battle of San Jacinto won Texas's freedom from Mexico.

Antonio López de Santa Anna (1794–1876) was a general and president of Mexico. His forces defeated Americans at the Alamo during the Texas Revolution.

James Polk (1795–1849) was the 11th president of the United States. At his urging, the U.S. Congress approved a declaration of war against Mexico.

Benito Juárez (1806–1872) was a liberal reformist president of Mexico who was replaced with Emperor Maximilian by Napoleon III. He was reelected after Maximilian's downfall.

Porfirio Díaz (1830–1915) was a Mexican general, president, and dictator. Under his rule, he opened the doors to foreign investment in Mexico's mines, plantations, and oil fields.

Victoriano Huerta (1854–1916) was a dictatorial president of Mexico. When he refused to give up power, U.S. president Woodrow Wilson sent troops to Veracruz, leading to Huerta's resignation.

Venustiano Carranza (1859–1920) opposed American intervention in Mexico, notably the U.S. occupation of Veracruz against Huerta and the military expedition to capture Pancho Villa on Mexican soil.

Francisco Madero (1873–1913) was president of Mexico from 1911 to 1913. Supported by revolutionaries Pancho Villa and Emiliano Zapata, he overthrew Porfirio Díaz and tried to reform Mexico's corrupt government.

Francisco "Pancho" Villa (1878–1923) was a Mexican revolutionary leader who fought for the rights of the poor, taking control of land and distributing it to local farmers.

Emiliano Zapata (1879–1919) was a leading military and social figure in the Mexican Revolution aimed at overthrowing President Díaz.

Álvaro Obregón (1880–1928) was a soldier and reformist president of Mexico who restored order to Mexico after years of political chaos and civil war that followed the revolution.

TIMELINE

Early 1300s

The Aztec settle in present-day Mexico City, where they establish the capital city of Tenochtitlán.

1521

Hernán Cortés and his Spanish forces conquer the Aztec Empire.

1795

Spain and the United States sign the Treaty of San Lorenzo, establishing U.S. borders at the Mississippi River and north Florida.

1836

February Santa Anna defeats Americans at the Alamo.

March Texans declare independence from Mexico.

April American forces defeat Santa Anna at the Battle of San Jacinto.

1837

March
The United States recognizes Texas independence.

1876

Porfirio Díaz assumes power in Mexico, where he rules for 35 years.

1910

The Mexican Revolution begins.

1917

A new constitution establishes social and economic rights of Mexicans.

1938

Mexican president Lázaro Cárdenas seizes foreign oil holdings in Mexico.

1810

The United States annexes western Florida.

1821

Mexico wins independence from Spain; Stephen F. Austin establishes a colony of Americans in Mexican territory.

1835

Santa Anna takes away Stephen F. Austin's right to self-government.

1845

December
The United States annexes Texas.

1846

The Mexican-American War begins.

1848

The Treaty of Guadalupe Hidalgo ends the Mexican-American War and grants the United States large areas of land in the West and Southwest.

1942–1964

The Bracero Program brings millions of Mexican workers to the United States.

1986

The Immigration Reform and Control Act attempts to limit illegal immigration to United States.

1994

The North American Free Trade Agreement goes into effect.

LIVING HISTORY

Primary sources provide firsthand evidence about a topic. Witnesses to a historical event create primary sources. They include autobiographies, newspaper reports of the time, oral histories, photographs, and memoirs. A secondary source analyzes primary sources, and is one step or more removed from the event. Secondary sources include textbooks, encyclopedias, and commentaries. To view the following primary and secondary sources, go to www.factsfornow.scholastic.com. Enter the keywords **United States and Mexico** and look for the Living History logo ∑¡.

∑¡ **The Hunt for Pancho Villa** The March 10, 1916, edition of Philadelphia's *Evening Public Ledger* reported on President Woodrow Wilson's order for the U.S. invasion of Mexico to hunt for Pancho Villa.

∑¡ **A Map of New Spain** Explorer Zebulon Pike published a map titled "A Map of the Internal Provinces of New Spain." It shows many Spanish-controlled territories, from the Gulf of Mexico in the east to the Colorado River in the west, as they stood in 1807.

∑¡ **Mexico's Seizing of Oil Properties** Mexican president Lázaro Cárdenas's seizure of oil properties in Mexico took control of Mexico's oil industry away from foreign investors and returned it to the Mexican government.

∑¡ **Operation Intercept** was an aggressive action to cut down on illegal drugs and immigrants coming into the United States from Mexico. Many newspapers reported on this controversial issue.

∑¡ **The Treaty of Guadalupe Hidalgo** The Treaty of Guadalupe Hidalgo ended the Mexican-American War and humiliated Mexico by forcing it to give up significant portions of land to the United States.

RESOURCES

Books

Burgan, Michael. *Ancient Aztecs*. New York: Children's Press, 2012.

Kent, Deborah. *Mexico*. New York: Scholastic, 2012.

Lange, Brenda. *Antonio Lopez de Santa Anna.* New York: Chelsea House, 2010.

Sorrels, Roy. *The Legend of the Alamo*. Berkeley Heights, NJ: Enslow Publishers, 2012.

Visit this Scholastic Web site for more information on the United States and Mexico: www.factsfornow.scholastic.com Enter the keywords United States and Mexico

GLOSSARY

agricultural (ag-ruh-KUL-chur-uhl) having to do with farming

aliens (AY-lee-uhnz) foreign people

annexed (AN-ekst) took control of a country or territory

debt (DET) money or something else that someone owes

deported (dih-POR-tid) sent someone back to the country from which that person came

dictatorship (dik-TAY-tur-ship) a form of government in which one ruler holds all power

economic (eh-kuh-NAH-mik) relating to the system of producing, distributing, and consuming goods and services

exported (EKS-por-tid) sent to a foreign country

immigrant (IM-uh-gruhnt) someone who comes from abroad to live in a country

imported (im-PORT-id) brought in from a foreign country

industrialized (in-DUHS-tree-uhl-ized) based around manufacturing companies and other businesses

inflation (in-FLAY-shuhn) a general increase in prices, causing money to be worth less

republic (ri-PUHB-lik) a form of government in which the people have the power to elect representatives who manage the government

siege (SEEJ) the surrounding of a place such as a building or a city in order to cut off supplies and wait for the people inside to surrender

tariffs (TAR-ifs) taxes charged on goods that are imported or exported

visas (VEE-zuhz) documents giving a person permission to enter a foreign country or stay there for a certain period of time

INDEX

Page numbers in *italics* indicate illustrations.

ABOUT THE AUTHOR

Nel Yomtov is an award-winning author of nonfiction books and graphic novels for young readers. He lives in the New York City area.